T0402897

Be a BEAR Expert

by
Noah Leatherland

BEARPORT
PUBLISHING

Minneapolis, Minnesota

Credits
All images are courtesy of Shutterstock.com, unless otherwise specified. With thanks to Getty Images, Thinkstock Photo, Adobe Stock, and iStockphoto.

Recurring – Milano M, pics five, MoonRock, tabako_ua, Stellar_bones, Perfect_kebab, Natalllenka.m, sycomore, vectorplus, The_Pixel. Doctor Character throughout – NotionPic. Cover – Szczepan Klejbuk, Perpis. 4–5 – ake_anupap, WildMedia. 6–7 – Alejandro-verges, Vaclav Sebek, Danica Chang. 8–9 – Erik Mandre, Green Mountain Exposure, Okyela. 10–11 – soyon, Tobias Grosskopf, Joanne Crawford, Mark Castiglia. 12–13 – PhotocechCZ, isabel kendzior. 14–15 – Chris Humphries, Somchai Siriwanarangson, Panompon Jaturavittawong. 16–17 – Alexey Suloev, Hung Chung Chih, Andrii PIATNYCHKA. 18–19 – Don Landwehrle, P Sahota, Sergey Uryadnikov. Don Landwehrle. 20–21 – Don Landwehrle, Aristov_tmb, Sergey Uryadnikov. 22–23 – Erik Mandre, Henk Bogaard.

Bearport Publishing Company Product Development Team
President: Jen Jenson; Director of Product Development: Spencer Brinker; Managing Editor: Allison Juda; Associate Editor: Naomi Reich; Associate Editor: Tiana Tran; Art Director: Colin O'Dea; Designer: Kim Jones; Designer: Kayla Eggert; Product Development Assistant: Owen Hamlin

Library of Congress Cataloging-in-Publication Data is available at www.loc.gov or upon request from the publisher.

ISBN: 979-8-88916-963-5 (hardcover)
ISBN: 979-8-89232-482-3 (paperback)
ISBN: 979-8-89232-118-1 (ebook)

For more information, write to Bearport Publishing, 5357 Penn Avenue South, Minneapolis, MN 55419.

CONTENTS

Meet the Biologist............4

A Bear's Body.................6

Sense and Climb 8

Know Your Bears...........10

Dinnertime..................16

Survival 18

Life Cycle...................20

Brainy Bears 22

Glossary....................24

Index 24

MEET THE BIOLOGIST

Hello! My name is Dr. Ursula Major, and I am a **biologist**. I have traveled the world to learn all about bears. They are amazing **mammals**!

4

Being a bear **expert** is a lot of work. My notebook is filled with everything I know about bears. Will you read it? Together, we can find out even more!

A BEAR'S BODY

There are eight different kinds of bears. These different **species** come in many different sizes and colors. Some bears are less than 40 inches (1 m) tall when standing. Others can reach more than 120 in. (3 m).

Polar bears are the largest species of bear.

6

All bears have fur. In cold places, they have thick layers of fur to keep them warm. Thinner layers of fur help bears stay cool in hot places.

Thick fur

Fur also keeps bears safe from being bitten by insects.

Thin fur

7

SENSE AND CLIMB

Bears have some of the strongest senses of smell in the world. The part of the brain that tells them about smells is five times bigger in a bear's brain than it is in a human's. This helps bears pick up the smell of food from miles away.

Sometimes, bears use sharp claws to dig for food and hunt the **prey** they smell. These claws are also good for climbing. They help bears grip onto tree trunks.

Claws

9

KNOW YOUR BEARS

Black and Brown Bears

Do you know your bears? Black bears live in the forests and mountains of North America. Brown bears are found in many different places, including Asia, Europe, and northwestern North America. Both bears are great tree climbers.

A black bear

A brown bear

Kodiak bears are the largest brown bears in the world.

Giant Pandas

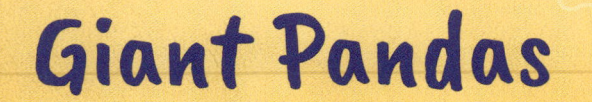

The cold mountains of China are home to giant pandas. There, the rainy, misty forests are full of a grassy plant called bamboo. Giant pandas spend about 12 hours a day just chowing down on bamboo!

Long wrist bones help giant pandas hold bamboo.

Polar Bears

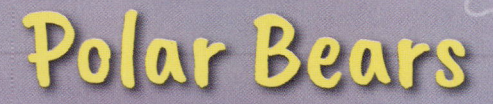

You can find polar bears in the freezing cold Arctic. They are very good swimmers. Large paws help polar bears paddle through the icy water.

Polar bears can close their nostrils to stop water from getting in their noses.

12

Sloth Bears

Sloth bears are found in the warm forests of South Asia. When sloth bears are hungry, they slurp termites and ants right out of their nests. Sloth bears also climb trees to eat honeycomb made by bees.

Sloth bears are very noisy eaters.

Spectacled Bears

Spectacled bears live in the Andes Mountains in South America. These bears get their name because colored fur around their eyes makes them look like they are wearing spectacles, or glasses.

Fur that looks like glasses

It is warm in the mountains where spectacled bears live. So, they have thin fur.

Sun and Moon Bears

Sun and moon bears are two other species of bears found in Asia. They get their names from the different patterns on their fur. Sun bears have a colored spot shaped like the sun, while moon bears have a crescent moon pattern.

A sun bear

A moon bear

DINNERTIME

Most bears are **omnivores**. This means they eat meat as well as plants. But some bears are **carnivores**. They eat only meat.

Brown bears wait by the water for salmon to leap out.

16

During winter, there is less food for some bears. These bears eat as much as they can when it is warm. Then, they do not eat all winter. They wait out the cold by sleeping in their dens instead.

A den is a cozy hidden spot where bears rest.

SURVIVAL

Bears have many ways to live and thrive in their **habitats**. Sometimes, they flip rocks over to look for bugs or other tasty snacks underneath. Bears can scratch themselves by standing and leaning their back against trees if they have an itch.

Bears **communicate** with one another by leaving scent trails.

18

There are times when bears will wander far from home. Luckily, they have a great memory and can easily find their way back. Bears can also remember the best places to find food.

Polar bears can easily travel across large areas of ice and water.

LIFE CYCLE

What is a bear's life cycle? Bears start life as babies known as cubs. Cubs stay with their mothers until they can survive on their own. For some cubs, this can take about two years.

A life cycle includes the different stages of an animal's life.

After leaving its mother, a bear usually lives alone. While some bears may come together to feed, they are mostly **solitary** creatures.

Bears in the wild can live for about 15 to 30 years.

BRAINY BEARS

From climbing trees to swimming long distances, bears can do so many brainy things! I hope you've enjoyed learning all about these amazing mammals.

You have just begun your bear adventure. There is so much more to learn about them. Continue to study. Soon, you'll be an expert, too!

GLOSSARY

biologist a person who studies and knows a lot about living things

carnivores animals that eat only meat

communicate to share information

expert someone who knows a lot about a subject

habitats places in the wild where animals normally live

mammals animals that are warm-blooded, drink milk from their mothers when they are young, and have fur

omnivores animals that eat both plants and animals

prey an animal that is hunted and eaten by another animal

solitary living alone

species groups that animals are divided into, according to similar characteristics

INDEX

bamboo 11
claws 9
cubs 20
forests 10–11, 13, 15
fur 7, 14–15

ice 19
mothers 20–21
mountains 10–11, 14
paws 12
trees 9–10, 13, 18, 22